AGW-6804

W9-CEA-971

Let The BROTHER Go If...

Coming "Let Go" Titles

Let The Sister Go if...
Let The Job Go if...
Let The (Grown) Kids Go if...

7.95

W

Phyllis R. Akers with Ms. Dupree

Let the BROTHER Go If...

Pines One Publications
Los Angeles

Library of Congress Cataloging-in-Publication Data

Akers, Phyllis R.,
Let the brother go if ... : 100+ reasons to walk away just when you think you can't! / Phyllis R. Akers ; with Miss Dupree.
p. cm. — (Let go books)
ISBN 1-890194-38-7
1. Mate selection. 2. Man-woman relationships. 3. Men—Psychology. 4. Single women—Psychology. 5. Dating (Social customs) I. Dupree, Miss, II. Title. III. Series.
HQ801 .A517 1999
646.7'7—dc21

99-37848
CIP

Books are available to organizations, corporations and professional associations at quantity discounts. For information, contact the sales department at Pines One Publications
(323) 290-1182; Fax (323) 295-3880; or E-mail Pinesone.worldnet.att.net

Text and cover design by Laurie Williams/A Street Called Straight
"Body Signs" illustration by TRUE/HeiroGraphiX

Printed in the United States of America
10 9 8 7 6 5 4 3 2 1
First Edition

Let The Brother Go if...

Can't smell his own sh_t

Cheating words

His _real_ thinking organ

Fondling hands

Dressed to impress—himself

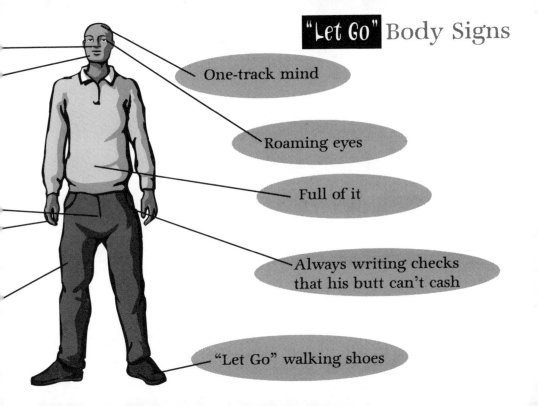

"Let Go" Body Signs

One-track mind

Roaming eyes

Full of it

Always writing checks
that his butt can't cash

"Let Go" walking shoes

Contents

Disclaimer
THIS IS NOT A MALE-BASHING BOOK

We know the majority of men are seeking a true love, just like women are.

Many of the comments in the book came from men. They themselves say women don't want the nice guy. They say women overlook the hardworking, down-to-earth man in favor of the smooth-talking player. They take the good man's kindness for weakness and beg to be with the one who uses and disrespects them. This book includes some of their tips for recognizing when to let the brother go.

This book will help the good brothers, because sisters won't be wasting time in unhealthy, dead-end relationships, and they'll be available for those good brothers. A sister won't have the built-up negativity from the prior relationship and if she lets go soon enough, you won't have to deal with her "baby's daddy."

Okay, okay, the book is a little hard on some brothers—the trifling ones. But none of this was invented; there are more than a few men folk who fit the profiles. If you're not one of them, don't take it personally. If you know one, help the brother get straight.

If women were more selective, there would be less divorce and fewer single mothers. This in turn would free up the divorce and family courts. Women wouldn't be subjected to stress and

abuse and would be able to raise more secure, healthier children. Our families would be stronger, our country would be stronger, we could help make the world a better place.
Let the brother go, and save the world!!

Introduction

Ending a relationship is tough. Scary, even, especially for women. If you let him go, will you miss your chance at true love? Statistics tell us there's a shortage of available men. But novels, TV shows, movies and advertisements all perpetuate the myth of happy endings with a "knight in shining armor." So maybe you think that if you just work on the frog, eventually he'll turn into a prince.

But be realistic. Sometimes it's difficult to just call a toad a toad and not fall victim to psychologically fooling ourselves. Countless experts and guests on talk shows point to low self-esteem and childhood issues as the roots of disharmony in bad relationships. So as a result, how many of us try to "fix" ourselves when what we really need to do is simply make the decision to let the brother go?

CHECK OUT THIS SCENARIO:

> WOMAN: *I found out my boyfriend is living with another woman. He says he's just helping her out and he really loves me. As soon as she has the baby, he's going to leave her. What should I do?*

> PSYCHOLOGY: *Your distress is brought on by feelings of abandonment you experienced as a child from a broken home. This situation simply reminds you of how your own father moved in and out of your life.*

> COMMON SENSE: *He ain't no good. Let the brother go!*

This book lets you know it's okay to say *adios* if the guy you're with is verbally and physically abusive, unfaithful, lazy, romantically inept, boring or just can't get along with your mother. It gives you support if you're on the fence, afraid of making a mistake. And it demystifies the hurtful beliefs some of us have that keep us stuck in relationships longer than necessary.

On these pages, you'll get all the reasons why you *can* let him go, along with suggestions on how to do it wisely and quickly.

Start your journey by taking the first quiz, "Is It Time to Leave?" If you're still not sure, take the second one, "Have I Been Fooling Myself Too Long?" If you have, we offer pearls of "Let Go Wisdom" from women who have accepted the challenge and "dumped with dignity."

From there, we introduce you to the "Dirty Dozen"— bad boys who try to pull the wool over your eyes with creative, seductive pickup lines. We'll show you how to see through the sugarcoated sleaze of introductions like "Your husband is one lucky guy," as he notices your ringless fingers, and "How do you choose a watermelon?" when he's got one in his grocery cart. From the places you're likely to meet these guys to how to show them the door, this section of the book serves as a field guide through the "jungle of jerks."

If you're a sister who's uncertain after you've already let him go, we offer "Afterthoughts" that are as comforting as Häagen-Dazs and a good movie. "For Brothers Only" gives men a two-minute warning of when it's coming. Finally, in "When to Keep the Brother," we give you tips on recognizing a good man and how to hold on to him.

There's something in this book for everyone. Whether you're on a first date or married and making the best of it, this portable reminder is the ammunition you need in the battle of the sexes.

This book is for him, so he knows what's coming; for a friend, so she'll keep you on course; and for you, so you can let the brother go if. . .

12 Excuses Women Use for Not Letting Go

EXCUSE #1: HE'LL CHANGE—ALL I HAVE TO DO IS HANG IN THERE A LITTLE LONGER.
REALITY: NOT! CHANGE IS SOMETHING YOU GET FROM A SLOT MACHINE.

EXCUSE #2: HE'LL DO UNTIL I FIND THE *RIGHT* PERSON.
REALITY: STOP LOOKING TO *FIND* THE RIGHT PERSON AND START LOOKING TO
   BE THE RIGHT PERSON.

EXCUSE #3: IT REALLY DOESN'T BOTHER ME WHEN HE FARTS OR DIGS IN HIS
   NOSE—IT'S NATURAL.
REALITY: IT'S NATURALLY DONE IN THE BATHROOM.

EXCUSE #4: IF HE TREATS HIS MOTHER GOOD, HE'LL TREAT ME THE SAME WAY.
REALITY: NOT IF HE'S A REAL MOTHER—(SHUT YOUR MOUTH).

EXCUSE #5: HE HAS POTENTIAL.
REALITY: YES, HE DOES IF HE'S IN HIGH SCHOOL. POTENTIAL STOPS AFTER 30.
        WHAT YOU SEE IS WHAT YOU GET!

EXCUSE #6: WHEN HE GETS SOME OF THIS, HE WON'T NEED NO OTHER.
REALITY: THAT'S WHAT THE OTHER FIVE WOMEN HE'S SEEING SAID TOO.

EXCUSE #7: WE REALLY GET ALONG; WE NEVER ARGUE.
REALITY: HE'S ARGUING WITH SOMEONE.

EXCUSE #8: HE'S A HOMEBODY.
REALITY: HE CAN'T GET CAUGHT TAKING YOU OUT.

EXCUSE #9: NO ONE ELSE WILL WANT ME.
REALITY: YOU CAN BE 300 POUNDS WITH FIVE KIDS AND SOMEONE WILL COME
          ALONG.

EXCUSE #10: HE'LL GROW TO LOVE ME.
REALITY: IF HE'S OVER 3 FEET TALL, IT'S TOO LATE.

EXCUSE #11: ALL MEN PLAY AROUND.
REALITY: NOT ALL MEN.

EXCUSE #12: THE SEX IS SOOOOO GOOD.
REALITY: EVEN THAT CHANGES.

Love or Misery?

Quiz I IS IT TIME TO LEAVE?

"Love isn't supposed to hurt." "You can be miserable by your-self." How many times have you heard these statements? We've all had men who bring us joy and pain. So how do you know when to call it quits?

1. Do you make excuses for him when he shows up late, forgets your birthday, or forgets to take his wallet so you have to pay for dinner?

Yes_____ No_____

2. Have you asked everyone you know—the mailman, the hairdresser, the mechanic, and the dentist—if you should let him go?

Yes_____ No_____

3. When an old girlfriend calls him, do you get fearful that he may go back to her?

Yes_____ No_____

4. Do you no longer care about his clothes, his friends, his car, and his mother?

Yes_____ No_____

5. Do you spend every waking moment wondering how he feels about you?

Yes_____ No_____

6. Does the way he moves his lips, breathes, walks, dresses irritate you beyond belief?

Yes_____ No_____

7. If a friend spots the two of you together, do you phone her the instant you get home and say, "It's not what you think?"

Yes_____ No_____

8. Is it hard to remember the last time he bought you something? Yes_____ No_____

9. Have you stopped reading his horoscope?

Yes_____ No_____

10. Does he introduce you as a "friend"?

Yes_____ No_____

11. Does your dog or cat hate him too?

Yes_____ No_____

12. Have you stopped dressing alike?

Yes_____ No_____

IF YOU ANSWERED "YES" TO:

> **0 questions:** Pass this book on to another sister; you don't need it.
>
> **1-2 questions:** Turn the page and take Quiz II.
>
> **3-5 questions:** Let the brother go soon.
>
> **6-12 questions:** Go straight to page 28.

Quiz II HAVE I BEEN FOOLING MYSELF TOO LONG?

When it's good, it's so good and when it's bad, it's too bad. Need some wisdom? Here's another quiz for those who are still not quite sure if you need to let the brother go.

1. At dinner, are you looking around at other couples having meaningful conversation wishing it were you?

Never   Sometimes   Always

2. Are you on a rescue mission—rescuing him from his clothes, bad friends, bad job, the world?

Never   Sometimes   Always

3. Have you stopped pretending you like watching sports?

Never   Sometimes   Always

4. Do you only receive flowers from him when he wants to make up?
Never   Sometimes   Always

5. Does a trip to his in-laws bring about nausea?
Never   Sometimes   Always

6. Does he apologize in a sexual manner?
Never   Sometimes   Always

7. Is the bedroom the only place he says "I love you?"
Never   Sometimes   Always

8. Is he asking for space—space from you, space from the relationship, any kind of space?
Never   Sometimes   Always

9. Does he handle the remote control more than you do?
Never   Sometimes   Always

10. When you're out with him, do you forget you *go out* with him?

Never   Sometimes   Always

11. Do his friends look better to you than he does?

Never   Sometimes   Always

12. Have you stopped buying "just because" cards?

Never   Sometimes   Always

IF YOU ANSWERED "ALWAYS" TO:

> **0 questions:** You're the envy of most women.
> **1-2 questions:** You might want to look at page 117.
> **3-5 questions:** Start turning the page.
> **6-12 questions:** This book was written just for you.

"Let Go" Wisdom

Letting go takes courage. Letting go takes guts. Letting go takes wisdom. But take heart, you are not alone. The trauma of letting go continues to be a hardship for women in BAD relationships. So before you start your journey, take a moment to gather your wits with some sisterly pearls of wisdom.

✔ Do it for yourself.
✔ Lock the door after he leaves.
✔ Fluff yourself up.
✔ Watch *Oprah.*
✔ Pick the right location for it (preferably with good lighting).

✔ Get your hair done.
✔ Tell him to keep it a secret.
✔ Make him pay his parking tickets first.
✔ Call in his IOUs.
✔ Cancel your IOUs.
✔ Take him off your car insurance.
✔ Get life insurance.
✔ Get your key back.
✔ Get your credit card back.
✔ Get your hair care products back.
✔ Get your CDs back.
✔ In fact, get all your stuff back <u>first</u>.
✔ Get rid of all the sentimental cards, tickets and gifts he gave you, but keep the jewelry—you might need to pawn it for a little pocket change later.

✔ Do mean it.
✔ Change your phone number or add that special phone ring feature signaling his calls.
✔ Tell your friends the two of you are no longer going out. You know they will keep you straight.
✔ Use an ex you never got over as an excuse.
✔ Take his number off your speed dial.
✔ Record it in your journal.
✔ Remember talk is cheap.
✔ Break ties with his family.
✔ Take your mother on a vacation.
✔ Remove his pictures from your purse, dresser and desk.
✔ Get a new hairstyle.
✔ Buy yourself the piece of jewelry he never would.
✔ Join a singles ministry.

✔ Learn a new hobby.
✔ Renew your commitment to your faith.
✔ Go to Jamaica—it worked for Stella.
✔ Buy the video "What's Love Got to Do with It?" for inspiration.

DON'TS

✘ Don't stumble over your words.
✘ Don't call Susan Taylor.
✘ Don't cry.
✘ Don't do it on a great-hair day.
✘ Don't pretend to like his family and friends anymore.
✘ Don't go to the restaurants that know you as a couple.
✘ Don't believe his hype.
✘ Don't end by saying, "Let's be friends."

✖ Don't tell him while he's cleaning his gun.
✖ Don't wing it—practice makes for a perfect exit.
✖ Don't broadcast your plans.
✖ Don't tell his mother first.
✖ Don't give him a copy of this book.
✖ Don't listen to Luther Vandross records.
✖ Don't answer his pages.
✖ Don't listen to his friends.
✖ Don't take collect calls.
✖ Don't backslide.
✖ Don't forget the past.
✖ Don't reach for the Häagen Dazs to get over it.
✖ Don't play old love songs that remind you of him.

SONGS FOR INSPIRATION

"CALL TYRONE" ERIKA BADU

"HIT THE ROAD JACK" RAY CHARLES

"SCORNED WOMAN" R KELLY

"IT'S TIME TO MOVE ON" SPARKLE

"I WILL SURVIVE" GLORIA GAYNOR

"WE'VE COME TO THE END OF OUR ROAD" GLADYS KNIGHT AND THE PIPS

"NEW ATTITUDE" PATTI LABELLE

"CONTROL" JANET JACKSON

5 Breakup Myths

BEING SINGLE IS A NIGHTMARE.

Nightmares come from spicy foods, and are generally on Elm Street. Is Freddie Kruger a friend of yours? If not, don't worry.

NOW I'LL HAVE SO MUCH SPARE TIME.

You had spare time while he was cheating. Spare time is like spare change—nobody has any.

WE'RE GOING TO SEE EACH OTHER AS FRIENDS.

What this means is that he's free to have his cake and eat it too. Cut the emotional ties so you can really move on, girl.

I'LL NEVER MEET A NICE MAN.

NOT TRUE. Besides, you thought he was nice once too. Take the time you need to heal, and get back in the race!

MY FAMILY AND FRIENDS WILL NEVER UNDERSTAND.

They didn't have to kiss him.

The Bright Side

Now you'll have time to do all the things you've been putting off (like taking a class, traveling, meeting other people, etc.), and you may even meet Mr. Right while doing them.

You can stop pretending to care which teams make the playoffs.

You can get reacquainted with your remote control.

You can pass gas when you feel like it.

You can wear rollers again.

You don't have to shave for a while.

You'll have more money.

You can order onion rings.

You can stop hanging out with his sister.

You can pawn the jewelry he gave you.

You can listen to your own music.

You can stop buying beer.

You can wear your comfortable underwear again.

You can stop pretending to like football.

The Dirty Dozen

and then some

12

So you've made mistakes in the past. You always seem to pick the wrong brother, and you can't understand why. You have great taste. You can walk into a boutique and immediately you're drawn to the classiest, most beautiful, most expensive thing in the shop. But when it comes to men, you always pick that irregular brother that doesn't fit anyone.

Are you tired of factory rejects? Sick of seconds? Would you like some quality goods? Well, since men don't come with tags that say "Passed by inspector #12," here is a guide to help you recognize quality when you see it.

Disguise #1:
Dream Come True

Profile: Packaged well—nice clothes, great car, fancy words.

Catch phrases: "I love being with you 24/7." "I'm really starting to like you."

Words they use to keep you hooked: They have visions of grandeur for the two of you. "Maybe we can take a cruise this summer." "I like family, that's important to me." "You know, you remind me of my mother."

What they really mean: I can hang here for a little while.

Where they're found: Black Expo's, conferences, professional office, a friend's house—all the places you think you would meet a great guy.

Mannerisms: Makes you think he really wants to be with you. Starts off cooking for you, paying for dinner, meeting your family and friends. He always wants to be with you. Calls you several times a day. He's always willing to help. He'll wash your car. He'll walk your dog. He'll even do your laundry. He'll do whatever he has to, to get what he wants. And I think you know what that is. Let's put it this way: He won't respect you in the morning.

Why we enter/stay in this relationship: We think these are great guys.

Prescription: Dose of reality. Prince Charming is only found in books.

Disguise #2:
Chocolate Fudge Sundae

Profile: Charismatic, seductive, debonair, sweet-talking, smooth-dancing.

Catch phrases: "I just like the way you...think, look, wear those clothes, talk..." (Just about everything you do is likable.) "Your husband is one lucky man."

Words they use to keep you hooked: "I like your hairstyle." "You sure know how to wear those clothes." You feel like you're having the best time of your life when you're with them. You're on the date from heaven. Enjoy this brother today, because tomorrow he may never call—at least not for six months till he's ready to have fun again. This guy gives you the Cinderella syndrome. They never talk about anything negative. He has the perfect job, family, etc. But you never get to know him long enough to know what he does.

What they really mean: I can't believe she's buying this stuff.

Where they're found: Vacation spots, the club, "errand" locations like the post office, grocery store, Kinko's, cleaners, gym. Places where you don't look your best, yet they tell you you look "fine."

Mannerisms: Looks you straight in the eye while talking his sweet talk. Loves to show his teeth. Loves to cuddle and hold hands. You kiss and fondle, but may never even have sex (he's not around long enough). He gives you a nickname like "Sweetie" or "Cutie," because he could easily mistake you for another one of his women. He leans towards you when he talks, but when *you* start talking, he pulls back and ignores you because he's really not trying to hear what you have to say. Always flirting with other women when he's with you—the waitress, the store clerk, the mail woman—every woman is open game. Looks good in his clothes. You never go to his house, and he never stays long at yours. You're always out and about doing things. Don't feel bad, he treats his guy friends the same way.

Why we enter/stay in this relationship: His lies are music to our ears.

Prescription: Go on a low-sugar diet—find a meat-and-potatoes guy.

Disguise #3:
Iceman

Profile: Emotionally unavailable, aloof, slick.

Catch phrases: "I'm cool." "I'm not hurt." "I can handle it." "It's not you, it's me."

Words they use to keep you hooked: "You're not like the other women I've known." "I could learn to trust you." "It's not easy for me to open up."

What they really mean: I'm so coldhearted, no one can hurt me.

Where they're found: Car wash, malls, record stores.

Mannerisms: Check out his walk, he swaggers. He wears sunshades at all times. His jewelry is always ever-present but tasteful. His clothing is impeccable. He has more hair care products than you do. He's always checking himself out. He's got an early-warning alarm on his feelings. If he feels himself getting too close, he'll pull up. The only time he'll get close is if it's cold outside. He's constantly sending out mixed signals that make you think you have a future together, but withdraws once you really start to like him. This is the guy you date for two years and then he gets married on you.

Why we enter/stay in this relationship: The challenge.

Prescription: Turn up the thermostat with someone else.

Disguise #4:
The Player

Profile: Shares himself with more than one woman.

Catch phrases: "I'm not interested in a commitment—but we're cool—right?" "Whatcha doing around midnight?" "I'll be by your place later." (Later may be two days from now.)

Words they use to keep you hooked: "We both have our own goals, rights." "A man is different from a woman—I know you're mature enough to understand that."

What they really mean: I'd like to do you if I don't have anything better to do.

Where they're found: Almost always in nightclubs, bars, concerts. But never ever in church.

Mannerisms: Reachable by pager, voice mail or cellular

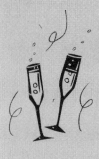

phone only. Doesn't address you by name; calls you "Boo," "Sweetie," "Baby"...because he can't afford to call you by the wrong name. This one is only available on the spur of the moment. Says he likes to keep it loose. He'll never make an appointment. Says spontaneity is the spice of life. If he likes you, he'll give you his mother's number. But she doesn't know where he is either. His address book is his most prized possession. Uses his car as both a lure and a home. He doesn't really lie, he just doesn't tell the truth—"You never asked if I was married."

Why we enter/stay in this relationship: We think we're the one that will really get him. Or we tell ourselves we're just having fun until someone else comes along.

Prescription: Unless he's a doctor, cut the wireless connection.

Disguise #5:
The Friend

Profile: Waiting for his chance to make a move.

Catch phrases: "You deserve someone better." "You can always count on me."

Words they use to keep you hooked: "No matter what, we'll always be friends." "Friends make the best lovers." "Girl, we go too far back to let anything come between us."

What they really mean: You let those other guys have some, why not me?

Where they're found: School, church, your mama's house.

Mannerisms: He takes you out on casual dates. If you have kids, they love him. He doesn't feel the need to impress you because you've known each other too long. He spends countless hours at your house. Gifts consist of food for you to cook. Look for a balloon and a card on your birthday. He thinks that since other men dogged you, he's *got* to be better, so why make an effort?

Why we enter/stay in this relationship:
We think it's safe.

Prescription: Platonic relationship?
—that's what friends are for.

Disguise #6:
The Dreamer
a.k.a. "Mr. Potential"

Profile: The man you hope will become better than he was when you met him.

Catch phrases: "I know everything is going to be alright as soon as..." Some miracle of God is what it normally takes.

Words they use to keep you hooked: "I just need you to have a little faith in me." "I want a woman who can share my dreams."

What they really mean: Maybe she'll let me crash here for a little while.

Where they're found: Community colleges, trade schools, free events.

Mannerisms: He's always getting ready to do something. He resents any questions about his ambition. He uses promises like toilet paper. He tries to convince you that you're crazy if you ever doubt him. He's a dream merchant and he'll sell you a bill of goods. He'd rather dream than sleep, and rather sleep than work.

Why we enter/stay in this relationship: We're fond of fairytales.

Prescription: Wake up!

Disguise #7:
The Artist
—and I'm not talking about the one formerly known as Prince

Profile: He's a starving artist of some kind just waiting for someone to notice.

Catch phrases: "If only I could sell one...baby, we'd be OK." "You inspire me." "I'm more sensitive than most men." "My temperament can't handle a regular job." "I'm self-employed."

Words they use to keep you hooked: "It takes a special woman to be with a man like me." "I know you understand me." "I'm a free spirit."

What they really mean: This line works on most women.

Where they're found: Bookstores, New Age shops, coffee-houses, Amway or some other sales meeting.

Mannerisms: He wears offbeat clothes. He always wears a hat. He smells like incense. He thinks Jimi Hendrix was the greatest man that ever lived. He'll take you on incredible highs—like when he's reading you poetry. And incredible lows—like when he asks you for the money to pay his phone bill. Even his family doesn't understand him, and they won't let him in the house either.

Why we enter/stay in this relationship: Romance seems to make more sense than finance. We feel we've invested too much energy, money, etc. to leave. You gave up on your dream, so you help your partner attain his. Only problem is, you seem to be doing all the work.

Prescription: Lose him—find a masterpiece.

Disguise #8:
The Holiday Bandit

Profile: Absent on birthdays, anniversaries, holidays—just about any day that's special.

Catch phrases: "I wanted to be there but..." "It's just another day, right?"

Words they use to keep you hooked: "I don't need a holiday to show you I care." "I'm still going to get you something, take you out when I get a chance—I haven't forgotten."

What they really mean: I had to be with my wife and kids.

Where they're found: These brothers are everywhere.

Mannerisms: As the holiday approaches, you don't see or hear from him. And when he surfaces, it's with an excuse that's loaded with so much drama you forget what holiday it was. Excuses like: "I was in the hospital. They thought it was a heart attack. I didn't call because I didn't want to worry you." Or: "You won't believe this, but the police stopped me because my taillight was out and then arrested me for outstanding parking tickets. So you know where I spent my night." Or: "My mother was sick."

Why we enter/stay in this relationship: We figure any man is better than none at all, plus you met him after a holiday.

Prescription: Celebrate with someone else!

Disguise #9:
The Harmless Nerd

Profile: At first he's adorable, eccentric, offbeat and intelligent. But then he changes into a weirdo.

Catch phrases: "Have you ever thought about how..." (some real thought-provoking question that entices you to want to continue talking to find the answer).

Words they use to keep you hooked: "Gee, I never did this before. But you can teach me." "I'll never find another woman like you."

What they really mean: I'm so weird I hope she thinks it's cute.

Where they're found: Computer stores, bookstores, libraries, high-tech conferences, college campus.

Mannerisms: His clothes are a little shoddy. He's clean but not well manicured. He usually wears glasses. And he is often better looking than he knows. He's usually inexperienced. And he could become obsessed. He's very insecure and at some point he'll say something that scares you. That's your cue to run. Run like the wind.

Why we enter/stay in this relationship: Trying not to be superficial.

Prescription: Try judging this book by its cover.

Disguise #10:
Mr. Possessive

Profile: Clings to outdated male/female roles. Arrogant, egotistical and know-it-all.

Catch phrases: "I want to take care of you." "Where you going?" "It better not be with Shanekwa—she got a big mouth." "Who was that on the phone?" "You shouldn't mind if you have nothing to hide."

Words they use to keep you hooked: "See, you couldn't handle this by yourself." "Face it, I'm better at some things than you are."

What they really mean: I'll kick your butt if you make me mad.

Where they're found: Police stations, personal ads, corporate offices, on the sidelines of clubs or parties.

Mannerisms: He always knows what's best for you. He

insists on ordering your meals, your drinks, your everything. He may start by asking you to wear certain things. He can see things that you can't, or so he says. His mantra is, "If you really loved me, you'd let me have my way." He convinces you that you need no one else but him. He won't stop until he's involved in every aspect of your life. And anyone who doesn't like him, doesn't want you to be happy. Except you're not happy with him. If he's so hooked on control, he should be a crossing guard. Then he can tell people which way to go.

Why we enter/stay in this relationship: You might not believe this, but some of us are flattered by the attention.

Prescription: The Emancipation Proclamation was signed in 1863—set yourself free!

Disguise #11:
The Wounded Man
a.k.a. "Mr. Pitiful"

Profile: Self-pity lifestyle.

Catch phrases: About the world: "Everything happens to me." About his wife: "We got together right after high school. She's been there for me, but I'm not in love with her." "We don't have sex anymore." "She doesn't understand me." About you: "No one understands me like you."

Words they use to keep you hooked: "I won't be with her much longer." "I never felt as close to her as I feel to you." "I need you."

What they really mean: I'm looking for a freak; my wife is too conservative.

Where they're found: At the office, the movies, the drugstore (usually buying tampons).

Mannerisms: He is so very needy. He makes you feel like you are saving his life. He has you wondering where he would be without you. He is a martyr and you're his savior. He's got you believing that one day soon it will be just the two of you. His favorite song is "Part-time Lover." He has you feeling noble for waiting for him, and he's convinced you that your friends and family are wrong about him. (Yeah, right!)

Why we enter/stay in this relationship: The same reason you took that puppy home from the pound. You think you can change his luck, until you find out why his wife really left him, why he didn't get the promotion—it's because he has no ambition.

Prescription: Physician, heal thyself!

Disguise #12:
Handyman-to-the-Rescue

Profile: Has a box full of tools that have never been used.

Catch phrases: "Can I use, borrow or have. . .?" "I live for today."

Words they use to keep you hooked: "Leave everything to me." "I've got your back." "I can fix anything."

What they really mean: I hope I can get a couple of home-cooked meals before you realize I can't fix anything.

Where they're found: Gas stations, hardware stores, outside work.

Mannerisms: He's always helpful. He will never ever let you have something done professionally. If he can't do it himself, he knows somebody who can. Whatever you do, don't let him or any of his friends near your plumbing, your car, your hair. His car and telephone are held together with duct tape. He patches the holes in his relationship too.

Why we enter/stay in this relationship: Some of us find clumsiness endearing. We convince ourselves his contributions to the household are as valuable as a paycheck. Having a dependent man often makes women think they are in control of the relationship. They feel that if they control the money, they control the man.

Prescription: Find a professional.

Disguise #13:
Ol' G.
a.k.a. "Mr. Has Been"

Profile: Interesting conversation, but stops at the '80s. May be an old flame.

Catch phrases: "I used to. . ." (this is OK if he's 80 years old). "My ex-wife got everything." "Remember when. . ."

Words they use to keep you hooked: Great stories about the job he used to have, the pro team he almost signed with, the car he used to drive.

What they really mean: I hope you think I'm still somebody important.

Where they're found: Bowling alleys, bars, school reunions, the gym.

Mannerisms: Still trying to figure out what he wants to be when he grows up. Can't recover from his divorce.

He still drives a "Z" and still does the funky chicken. If he still wears platforms, run—you can outrun him.

Why we enter/stay in this relationship: Trying to recapture our youth. If he's an old flame, time may have dulled our memory of why we broke up in the first place. Does the phrase "Revisionist History" ring a bell?

Prescription: Treat him like the Y2K delemma—upgrade!

The Abuser

THE "MUST LET GO" BROTHER

There are some men you cannot have anything to do with. If you want to deal with a Casanova or support a User, help yourself. But some types are dangerous and you should run, not walk away.

SIGNS TO RECOGNIZE

These include physical and verbal abuse. The most obvious physical abuse is fights. Slaps, pushes and shoves do count. Even if your partner never lays a hand on you but you alter your behavior because you are afraid of what he might do, this is still a volatile relationship. Verbal abuse is demeaning, embarrassing and unnecessary. Name-calling, threats and cursing are all verbal abuse. Sisters have been known to let loose with tongue-lashings as well. Don't belittle, deceive or put down your man. Let him go if you feel that way.

PRESCRIPTION

You've heard it a thousand times: If he hits you once, he'll do it again. Each time will only get worse. There is no certain type; he can be well educated or unemployed, super-fine or The Mummy's twin. An abusive man has a problem, and unless he gets help to deal with it, you need to let him go. This type of relationship is harmful to your self-worth as well as to your body (remember Halle Berry's revelation of hearing loss due to an abusive relationship?). You could ultimately end up dead. If you don't break the cycle, your children will witness this activity and think this is the norm and perpetuate it with their mates. He may be apologetic and contrite, but you must stick to your guns.

HOW TO LET HIM GO...

This won't be easy. This person generally thinks of you as his possession and is not willing to let you go. Many domestic fatalities occur when the woman tries to leave. Have a plan of action, put money aside if you can, and don't broadcast your plans. You may have to pursue legal action. But beware, a restraining order is just a piece of paper and cannot keep someone away from you. It determines what happens to the person if they violate the order, but it does not keep them from violating the order. If you must leave a situation like this, go to the house of a friend or relative, preferably a man, or have them stay with you. This sounds chauvinistic, but this is a life-and-death situation and you have no time for feminist politics. The abuser is less likely to bother you with others around. You may have to leave your home or even leave town. Material things can be replaced, and you can find another job. Your life cannot be replaced.

50+ Signs of a Really *Bad* Date

❝ WHEN SOMEONE REVEALS THEMSELF TO YOU, BELIEVE THEM. ❞

—MAYA ANGELOU

How many times have you heard callers ask for advice on a talk show, or read sob stories in the *Ebony* Advisor, and you just wanted to shout "WAKE UP!"? How many books like *10 Stupid Things Women Do to Mess Up Their Lives* or *Never Satisfied: How and Why Men Cheat* do women have to read to find out why they end up in doomed relationships with brothers they never should have hooked up with in the first place? Recognizing the sign of a bad date, bad relationship or bad marriage is critical to letting go. Some signs will be evident after the first date. If you see them, don't bother with a second. The clues below will probably let you know you don't have Mr. Right.

Let the Brother Go If...

☞ HE SAYS, "YOU'RE NUMBER ONE. EVERYONE ELSE COMES BEHIND YOU."
This isn't the Kentucky Derby.

☞ HE CAN'T REMEMBER YOUR NAME.

☞ HE WANTS YOU TO MEET HIS PSYCHIC FRIENDS.
You remember what happened to Dionne Warwick.

☞ HE MISSPELLED YOUR NAME ON YOUR VALENTINE CARD.
He needs "Hooked on Phonics."

☞ HE DOESN'T SHOW UP ON TIME, AND WHEN HE DOES, HE BRINGS HIS FRIENDS.
Enough said.

☞ HE'S BEEN A GUEST ON THE *JERRY SPRINGER* SHOW.
No explanation needed.

☞ HIS PHONE KEEPS RINGING
Someone is checking on him.

☞ HE USES EBONICS AS STANDARD ENGLISH.
And what be wrong wi' dat?

☞ HE CAN'T REMEMBER HOW MANY JOBS HE'S HAD IN THE LAST YEAR.
Can he remember his way home?

☞ HE STILL WEARS A JHERI CURL
Think about your pillowcases.

☛ HE LIVES WITH HIS MOTHER.
Your place is next!

☛ HE SPENDS MORE TIME IN THE MIRROR THAN YOU DO.
Ask to use his eyeliner.

☛ HIS FRIENDS TELL YOU YOU'RE MAKING A MISTAKE.
And they like him.

☛ HE CALLS YOU COLLECT FROM PRISON.
Dump him next visitors' day.

☛ YOU DON'T SEE HIM ON WEEKENDS.
His wife doesn't like double dating.

☛ HIS EX IS STALKING YOU.
This is not the time to stand by your man.

☞ **THE FIRST DATE IS AT HIS HOUSE.**
And he charged admission.

☞ **HE DISAPPEARS ON HIS PAYDAY.**
And so does his check.

☞ **THE LIQUOR STORE OWNER KNOWS HIM BY NAME.**
And so does his bookie.

☞ **YOUR DOG DOESN'T LIKE HIM.**
It takes one to know one.

☞ **HE WON'T WEAR A CONDOM.**
No glove, no love.

☞ **HE FORGETS YOUR BIRTHDAY.**
And you were born on December 25th.

☛ HE WEARS HIS PANTS BELOW HIS WAISTLINE.
Well, if he's making a million doing it, then it's OK.

☛ YOUR MOTHER DOESN'T LIKE HIM.
Don't be hasty, that could be a plus.

☛ HE HITS YOU ONCE.
He'll hit you again, and again, and again—get the picture?
Nothing funny about that.

☛ HE ONLY GIVES YOU HIS PAGER NUMBER.
His wife answers his phone.

☛ HE ALWAYS WANTS TO GO DUTCH.
Tell him to move to Holland.

☛ HE'S MARRIED.
He's gone.

☛ HE ASKS YOU TO CO-SIGN FOR A LOAN OR WANTS TO BORROW YOUR
CREDIT CARD.
Give him bus fare and a hearty heave-ho.

☛ YOU CATCH HIM IN A LIE.
That's the first one of many to follow.

☛ HE'S RECOVERING FROM ANYTHING—CRACK, ALCOHOL, GAMBLING...
And you are recovering from bad relationships.

☛ HE CAN'T KEEP A JOB.
Then he can't keep you.

☛ HE DOESN'T LIKE TO TRY ANYTHING NEW.
He's stuck in stupid.

☛ HE NEEDS TO BORROW YOUR CAR FREQUENTLY.
They try harder at Avis.

☛ HE BLAMES THE WHITE MAN FOR EVERYTHING.

Sure, cheating is the white man's fault.

☛ HE'S MISSING FRONT TEETH.

Teeth are not optional.

☛ HE NEVER TALKS ABOUT HIS PAST—PAST JOB, PAST GIRLFRIEND.

Then he's past tense.

☛ HE'S OVER 35 AND NEVER BEEN MARRIED.

If he's so hot, why has everybody else missed it?

☛ HE DOESN'T PAY CHILD SUPPORT.

Call Ricki Lake.

☛ HE DISLIKES ALL YOUR FRIENDS.

And they dislike him.

☞ HE WANTS TO BORROW MONEY EARLY IN THE RELATIONSHIP.
So you make an early withdrawal.

☞ HE'S DATED EVERYONE AT WORK.
Don't let him punch your clock—he's punched in too many times.

☞ HE SEEMS OK, BUT ALL HIS FRIENDS ARE FREAKS, WEIRDOS OR LOSERS.
He's probably their leader.

☞ HE DOESN'T VOTE OR PAY TAXES.
It's only a matter of time for this brother. Can you say "garnished"?

☞ HE PRESSURES YOU FOR SEX.
"Please, baby, baby, please..." Sound familiar?

☛ YOUR DATES ONLY CONSIST OF SEX.
That's too much dessert.

☛ YOU THINK HE HAS "POTENTIAL"
Wait until he blooms.

☛ YOU THINK HE DRINKS, DOES DRUGS OR IS CHEATING
You don't need a psychic for this one.

☛ YOU ALWAYS PAY FOR EVERYTHING
Tell him to call Tyrone.

☛ HE NEVER CALLS YOU.
Step away from the phone.

☛ YOU HEAR FROM HIM SPORADICALLY, AND WHEN HE DOES CALL,
HE WANTS TO SEE YOU RIGHT THEN.
Can you say "booty call"?

☛ HE HAS DOUBLE STANDARDS.

And now he's single. You must call before going to his place; he just shows up at yours. He can answer your phone; you can't answer his. Get the picture?

☛ HE WON'T TAKE YOU TO MEET THE FAMILY.

Someone's already met them.

☛ HE TELLS YOU TO LET HIM GO.

Duh!

Timing Is Everything

"Never Can Say Good-bye" is a song title. But is there really ever a good time to say "good-bye"? Yes! And the time is now, if the brother is working your last nerve. So preserve your sanity, self-esteem and nervous system, and consider the following times to say "farewell."

Holidays

It may seem cruel, but he'll see his family and friends during this time and they will comfort him. Plus he'll get some time off work to mope. And he won't be sad for long since everyone around him will be happy. See, this works out for both of you.

Birthday (his)

Save yourself some money. Give yourself a gift and let this brother go just before his birthday. And if you need strength to do this, remember the last birthday present he gave *you*.

Birthday (yours)

Get your gift first, then let him go.

Friday night

You know how brothers love to prepare for the weekend on Monday. You will really mess up his weekend by letting go on a Friday night. And if you let him go early, you'll still have time to catch Happy Hour.

Valentine's Day

Since most men could care less about this holiday, he won't be offended. In celebration of the day, wear red.

At a funeral

If you're looking for emotion from him, this may be the only time you'll see tears. Now, we know they won't really be for you, but you can tell your friends he cried when you told him. And exaggerate—you'll feel much better.

After he loses his job

You'll save a lot of money. Borrowing ruins any relationship.

After he paid for a vacation

Why not have one last treat on him? But give him the pictures.

After dinner

You'll be more confident on a full stomach. But you may have to raise your voice if it's a fast-food restaurant.

At the airport

Ensures a short good-bye.

At a party

You can get rid of one and find another at the same event. But wait till the DJ plays "Reasons."

At your place

In the doorway.

At his place

In the doorway.

Just before the police put him in the car

Tell him to "watch his head."

E-mail

Even if he doesn't have a computer.

Exit Lines

Composing the farewell speech is difficult. To avoid disastrous results, however, we've provided you with foolproof lines. Practice the lines for your situation until you can say them naturally. Now find your target, aim, and prepare for your Oscar.

To make your exit as easy as possible, take advantage of the collective wisdom of sisters everywhere. The following lines have been used by women for centuries. These have survived the test of time.

TIPS

Deliver it with a straight face.
Don't let him talk.
Be convincing.
Keep it short and simple.

AFTER THE FIRST DATE

"We really didn't connect."
"My boyfriend and I are getting back together."
"I'll call you when I get my test results back."
"I'm pregnant."
"Oil and water don't mix."
"My therapist thinks it's too soon for me to date."
"I'm joining a convent."

AFTER A FEW DATES

"I don't have time for a relationship right now. Let's be friends."

"Don't take it personally, but I just got out of a really bad relationship and I need time."

"I'm moving out-of-the-state next week."

"My other personality, Tanya, doesn't like you."

"Trust me, I'm so screwed up, you really don't want to be with me."

"I'm really a man."

"I've run out of my medication; I'll call you after I see my shrink."

IF YOU'RE IN A LONG-TERM RELATIONSHIP

"I need some space right now."
"I love you too much—it scares me!"
"Let's get married."
"Let's see other people."
"You're too good for me."
"I have to go into the witness protection program."
"I don't want to hold you back."
"We need to talk."

IF YOU'RE MARRIED

"I want to have three more kids."
"I'm quitting my job."
"I think we should join a commune."

"I maxed out all your credit. Can you get some more?"
"Insanity runs in my family."
"I never really liked you."
"I need to find myself."
"I'm pregnant and it's not yours."
"I know I should have told you this before we got married, but
"I really want to strip for your friends."

Exit Lines for the Dirty Dozen

Let Go of Dream Come True

You say, "I've been having nightmares about you."
"I'm psychic. I know what's coming."

Let Go of Chocolate Fudge Sundae

You say, "I'm tired of going to your girlfriends' baby showers."
"I wouldn't do this if you could remember my name."
"I want to move in with you."

Let Go of Iceman

You say, "You should find someone who really deserves you."
"I can't afford to buy you any more jewelry."

Let Go of The Player

You say, "The booty-call line has been disconnected."
"I think we're ready to move to the next level."
"Your wife, girlfriend and I are getting together next week."

Let Go of The Friend

You say, "Let's stop this before we ruin our friendship."
"At least we can say we tried."

Let Go of The Dreamer

You say, "You should be all that you can be. And I'll be all I can be, without you."
"One day I hope I'll say, 'You're the one I let get away.'"
"I want to quit my job and write."

Let Go of The Artist

You say, "Use this pain as inspiration."
"You're so deep I know you can understand this."

Let Go of The Holiday Bandit

You say, "Let's make every day a holiday."
"Let's celebrate being apart."

Let Go of The Harmless Nerd

You say, "We've grown apart."
"I think therapy could really help you."

Let Go of **Mr. Possessive**

You say, "If you want to train somebody, get a pet."
"You're always telling me what I can't handle. Well, what I can't handle is you."

Let Go of **The Wounded Man**

You say, "Your wife doesn't understand you and neither do I."
"You said we'll be together someday. Well, someday is when I'll see you again."

Let Go of **Handyman-to-the-Rescue**

You say, "If it ain't broke, don't fix it."
"Some things are better left to professionals."

Let Go of Ol'G.

You say, "Out with the old, in with the new."
"I didn't like you the first time either."

Process of Elimination

(THE IMPERSONAL APPROACH)

How you let the brother go is just as important as what you *say*. Let's say that the relationship has gotten so bad by now that you can't stand the sight of him. Or to meet with him would be a violation of the "restraining order." In these cases, the impersonal approach is appropriate.

Let Go with a Letter

Start with, "Dear John." In the first paragraph you should remind him how good you were. But in the second paragraph, you drop the bomb. And close by saying, "Let's not be friends."

Risk   He may never read it. So he'll keep calling you until you read it to him.

Etiquette tips

- Use half-sheet stationery to get to the point.
- Handwrite it.
- Check spelling and grammar. (You don't want his last memory to be of a woman who splits infinitives or is Ebonically challenged.)

- Choose your words carefully.
- Do not use a return address.

Let Go by Fax

This is a 21st-century approach. Faxing is not exactly classy but quick and cheap. Your friends may end up siding with him if they hear you were so coldhearted as to dump him via fax. However, if he's a workaholic, this is the only way.

Risk   Others may see it and it may never find its way to his desk.

Etiquette tips

- Use a cover page.
- Keep it short.
- Don't mark it "confidential" or "urgent."

Let Go by E-mail

Use this for the guy who likes cyber relationships.

Risk   He may reply with Melissa (no, not his new girlfriend, but the fatal e-mail virus).

Etiquette tips

- Put "Freedom" in the subject area.
- Keep it short. He shouldn't have to scroll through the verbiage.
- Text only. Don't attach a cute graphic.
- Delete him from your address book.

Let Go by Phone

It's inexpensive, readily accessible and cheap. Not to mention, it's about as close to in person as you can get. Unfortunately, he has an opportunity to say his final word.

Risk He might change your mind, hang up, or simply not believe you unless you say it face-to-face. You may hate the sound of his voice.

Etiquette tips

- Call from a call-blocking line.
- Do it alone—don't call the girls over for support.
- Ignore call waiting until you've gotten it out, then use it to get off the phone.

• Time yourself (20 minutes if he lives in your city; 10 if he's out-of-state).

• Call the phone company first and get that special-ring feature to denote his calls.

Let Go by Answering Machine

This method is for those long-winded sisters or for someone you've only gone out with for a short time. You only have 30 to 60 seconds to say it before you get cut off. Use this method just before you get on a plane to go out of the country for a few weeks. This method is definitely for the passive-aggressive type.

Risk His visiting mother may hear it.

Etiquette tips

- Script it out.
- Don't use a cell phone. (The crackly line may seem like you said, "I've given it a lot of thought and I want...this relationship.")
- Practice!

Let Go by Using Someone Else

Risk   Have you heard the phrase "kill the messenger"?

Etiquette tips

- Choose a good friend.
- Don't send your new boyfriend.
- Use his mother only in extreme cases.

Let Go with a Message in a Bottle

Risk You won't be able to get your deposit back.

Etiquette tips

Don't use a 40-ounce bottle.

Let Go with a Ouija Board

Risk You could become possessed.

Etiquette tips

Use a spirit you're familiar with.

"Let Go" Afterthoughts

Changing your mind is a woman's prerogative. But baby, you've got to learn to trust your feelings. Breakup remorse is normal, so recognize the following as simply normal reactions.

DID I MAKE A MISTAKE? No, you didn't. He made the mistake by losing you.

SHOULD I SLEEP WITH HIS BEST FRIEND? Not recommended, but don't rule it out.

HE'S MY BABY'S DADDY. Your baby may deserve a better daddy.

CAN WE JUST HAVE SEX? No. Find a new man for that. Don't you watch *Jerry Springer?*

HE'S MY BOSS—SHOULD I GET ANOTHER JOB? No. But keep a lawyer on retainer.

WILL HE LIE ABOUT ME? Probably.

SHOULD I STAY IN TOUCH WITH HIS MOTHER? Only to get her secret sauce recipe.

IS ANY OF MY UNDERWEAR MISSING? Lilac is his color.

DID HE REALLY DESTROY THAT VIDEOTAPE? I hear he's charging admission.

SHOULD I LET HIM SEE THE DOG? No, she's already got enough fleas.

IS HE DOING THE SAME THINGS WITH OTHERS THAT HE DID WITH ME? You knew he was a freak when you met him.

SHOULD I GIVE HIS RING BACK? No, but I'd have it appraised.

Should You Tell a Friend to Let Go?

We've all been in the situation where your sister or best friend is madly in love with someone who's no good for her. What should you do?

Some say stay out of it. If they break up, they may get back together and then she'll be mad at you—or worse, she'll think you're after him. So we say nothing and join in the conspiracy of silence that lets women be made fools of. How can you help a friend to let go?

Buy her this book.

Introduce her to someone nice.

Go to a play or a movie (not dinner—you'll just end up talking about men).

Buy her this book.

Take her shopping.

Pull out old yearbooks and photos—remind her she had a life before.

Buy her this book.

Treat her to a massage.

Reassure her that she did the right thing.

Buy her this book.

Rent *Waiting to Exhale*.

Go to a male strip show.

Oh yeah, buy her this book.

For Brothers Only

(WARNING SIGNS)

Unless you had a flaky woman, a breakup shouldn't come as a surprise. Just like a rocky road, there are always warning signs along the way. Here are signs to let you know the "thrill is gone." She's getting ready to let you go if:

- She stops wearing that sexy lingerie you like.
- She has a headache all the time.
- When you finally surprise her with something, she says "Thank you" with no sex attached.
- She takes interest in how she looks.
- She starts talking about a new friend—male.

- When she introduces you to people, she refers to you as her "friend."
- When you come back from a two-week trip, she says, "Back already?"
- She orders a double dessert at dinner.
- She starts hitting on your friends in front of you.
- You saw this book in her purse.
- She introduces you to girls you know she thinks you'd like.
- You get a card from the *Dating Game* and she referred you.
- She keeps humming "Breaking Up Is Hard To Do."
- She moves and leaves no forwarding address.
- The last thing she cooked you was a bag of potato chips.
- She names her dog after you.
- She sets your clothes on fire.
- She says she can't go out because she can't find a babysitter.

- She stops wearing the perfume you bought her.
- She goes to a wedding and doesn't invite you.
- She forgets your birthday.
- She tells you not to get her a Valentine's Day present.
- She calls and leaves messages when she knows you're not home.
- She suggests you spend more time at your place.

What should you do?

You rotten brothers should just promote lady #2 to the #1 spot.

You good decent brothers should accept it like a man and forge on, looking for your soulmate.

When to Keep the Brother...

This book cannot end without recognition for the many men that are worth your time, love and respect. Here are some clues to recognize a winner.

When he holds your hand in public.
When he lets you hold the remote.
When he listens.
When he brags about you to his friends.
When you come home and dinner is cooked.
When he remembers your birthday.
When he pumps your gas.
When your friends want him.
When your mother and father like him.

When he keeps you laughing.

When you gain a few pounds and he's not trying to get you in the gym.

When he wants to go to a family function—yours.

When he asks for directions.

When he sends you a note—just because.

When he picks up the phone hoping it was you.

When he wants to grow old together.

When he goes on a trip and brings you something back.

When he loves you more than you love him.

When he takes the trash out.

When he takes you to his church.

When you meet his family and they say, "We've heard so much about you!"

When he puts the seat down.

When he takes your kids to Disneyland.

When he dresses like you.

When he orders your dessert.

When he buys your mom a Mother's Day gift.

When he holds the umbrella over you when it's raining.

When he just wants to talk.

When your dog likes him.

When he turns off his pager.

When he'd rather be with you than watch the game.

When he nurses you when you're sick.

When he does any kind of shopping with you.

Second-Chance Brothers

Everyone deserves a second chance. How do you know that this brother isn't really telling the truth? Maybe he really *is* between jobs. Maybe he really *is* separated. Timing is everything. The Player you meet at 25 may be ready to settle down by 35. Let him go if you meet him at 25; keep him if you meet him at 35. Second-chance considerations:

—Do you have the same goals in life?

—Notice how he talks about past relationships. Does he take any responsibility? Or were problems always someone else's fault?

—Is he free to be with you now?

—Is he healthy? Does he take care of himself? A recovering alcoholic may make a good boyfriend, but how long has he been on the wagon—three days or three years?

—What do others say about him? You don't want to believe all hearsay, but comments from others who've known him longer than you could offer insights into his personality.

—Don't be hasty. Give yourself time to view him over the long term. Has he just been putting on his "best behavior" or are these really good characteristics of his natural personality?

IF YOU'RE GIVING HIM A SECOND CHANCE, ASK YOURSELF THE FOLLOWING:

—Is he still fine?

—Has he accumulated a lot of frequent flyer miles?

—Does he still give good gifts?

—Has he really changed?

"Let Go"

At-A-Glance

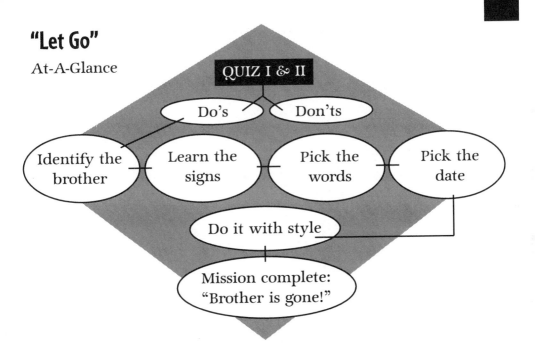

Acknowledgments

To my mother, who always has my back.
To my children, I'll always have your back.
To the brothers I didn't let go, but should have—thanks for the inspiration.
Thanks to the brother I didn't let go—thanks for keeping me.

—P.A.

Of course all thanks to God—I know it's a cliché, but I mean it. I also want to thank my husband, daughter, sisters and, of course, my mother, for their constant support.

Thanks to my friends—you know who you are. Thanks to the champions of my cause: Tom Joyner and Tavis Smiley. A special thanks to all the rotten brothers of the world for inspiring this book.

—Ms. D.

About the Authors

PHYLLIS R. AKERS is a native of Milwaukee, Wisconsin. She is a banker and bookseller and divides her time between Houston, Texas and Pine Bluff, Arkansas. She is the mother of three and is in process of birthing another baby—her first novel.

MS. DUPREE, a.k.a. JEDDA JONES RICHARDS left the corporate world in pursuit of a career in comedy. She has written for numerous television shows and for several successful comedians. She has been seen in numerous movies and sitcoms and still performs stand-up comedy across the country. Ms. Dupree can be heard every Wednesday on the Tom Joyner Morning Show.